IMAGES
of America

THE PIG WAR

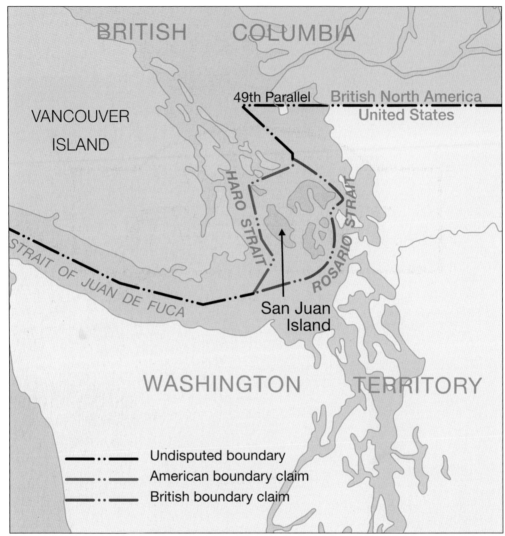

BRITISH COLUMBIA

VANCOUVER
ISLAND

49th Parallel British North America
United States

HARO STRAIT

ROSARIO STRAIT

STRAIT OF JUAN DE FUCA

San Juan
Island

WASHINGTON TERRITORY

——··—— Undisputed boundary
——··—— American boundary claim
——··—— British boundary claim

The Pig War crisis of 1859 flared 13 years after the Treaty of Oregon was signed because of a mapping error. In order to permit the British full possession of Vancouver Island as agreed (and which they had held since 1843), the boundary was drawn along the 49th parallel to the middle of the Strait of Georgia and southerly through the "channel" that divides Vancouver Island from the mainland. But there are actually three channels running through and around the San Juan Archipelago. When this was pointed out—after the treaty was drawn—Great Britain and the United States decided to hold the islands in dispute. This worked out on paper, but in the Pacific Northwest, it was quite another story.

ON THE COVER: Officers and seamen strike poses for the photographer aboard Her Britannic Majesty's Ship (HBMS) *Satellite*, probably in Esquimalt Harbor, northwest of Victoria on Vancouver Island. *Satellite* was a 21-gun steam corvette, the newest and largest of her class in the late 1850s. The ship was very much involved in the Northwest Boundary Survey and stood sentinel in Griffin Bay during the Pig War crisis. (San Juan Island National Historic Park.)

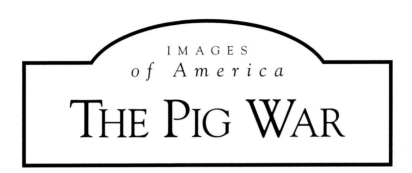

IMAGES
of America

THE PIG WAR

Mike Vouri

ARCADIA
PUBLISHING

Published by Arcadia Publishing
Charleston SC, Chicago IL, Portsmouth NH, San Francisco CA

Printed in the United States of America

Library of Congress Catalog Card Number: 2007943609

For all general information contact Arcadia Publishing at:
Telephone 843-853-2070
Fax 843-853-0044
E-mail sales@arcadiapublishing.com
For customer service and orders:
Toll-Free 1-888-313-2665

Visit us on the Internet at www.arcadiapublishing.com

For Julia.

CONTENTS

ACKNOWLEDGMENTS

I want to thank Supt. Peter Dederich and the staff and volunteers of San Juan Island National Historical Park for their support and friendship over the years; Dr. Julie K. Stein, archaeologist and director of the Burke Museum at the University of Washington; Jacilee Wray, Olympic National Park anthropologist, for her outstanding cultural affiliation study of the Salmon Banks fishery at South Beach; my mother and father, Sue and John Vouri, for their lifelong love and support; Ron Redding and Ron Toburen, buds till the end; and, as always, warm thanks to my wife and editor, Julia Vouri.

IMAGE ABBREVIATIONS:

British Columbia Archives—BCA
Beinecke Rare Book and Manuscript Library, Yale University—BRBML
Library of Congress—LOC
National Archives of Great Britain—NAGB
National Archives of the United States—NARA
Whatcom Museum of History and Art—WMHA

All images not otherwise credited are courtesy of the San Juan Island National Historical Park.

INTRODUCTION

In 1859, the United States and Great Britain nearly went to war over the shooting of a pig on San Juan Island.

The island today is known and loved by whale watchers, kayakers, bicyclists, time-share condo owners, and day-trippers. It is a 54-square-mile gem lying between Vancouver Island, British Columbia, and the rugged mainland of Washington state. The island is also home to San Juan Island National Historical Park, which was created by Congress in 1966 to commemorate the peaceful resolution of the Northwest Boundary Dispute between the United Kingdom of Great Britain and the United States.

The dispute is perhaps the best-known period in island history. But the park also encompasses a rich and diverse environment that cannot be separated from the island's 3,000-year human history. Long before the arrival of Europeans, the island sheltered a thriving culture attracted by its temperate climate, rich soil, abundant timber, and marine resources. These same attributes lured Spain, Great Britain, and the United States, each of whom explored, charted, and named the islands while staking claims to the Oregon Country—the present states of Washington, Oregon, Idaho, portions of Wyoming and Montana, and the province of British Columbia.

Spain had abandoned its claims by the mid-1790s, leaving the region to the British and Americans. Following the War of 1812, they signed a treaty that provided for a joint exploration and occupation of the Oregon Country and stipulated that possession of the region would be determined by "effective occupation," that is, the nation that established commerce and settlement would have the strongest claim. Although lucrative trade agreements and capital investments existed between the two nations, primarily on the Eastern Seaboard, trouble was brewing among those living in the Oregon Country. Americans considered the West Coast British colonies an affront to their "Manifest Destiny." The British believed they had a legal right to lands guaranteed by earlier treaties, explorations, and commercial activities of the Hudson's Bay Company (HBC).

The HBC, established on its namesake bay in 1670, acquired the rival North West Company in 1821, which included the Montreal-based company's facilities in the Pacific Northwest. One of those properties was Astoria, a fledgling fur post at the mouth of the Columbia River, which had been simultaneously purchased and taken as a prize of war by the Northwesters and the Royal Navy during the War of 1812. Three years later, the renamed Fort George post was shifted more than 70 miles upriver to become Fort Vancouver. As headquarters for a network of trading posts and agricultural stations throughout the Oregon Country, Fort Vancouver became the hub of a mercantile empire that expanded from furs to timber, fishing, and agriculture. In the face of a desultory U.S. settlement, the British through the late 1830s believed that these efforts gave them the right to the Oregon Country.

But starting in the late 1830s, the merits of the Oregon Country were being extolled by missionary organizations on both sides of the Atlantic. The result was a vast westward migration. By 1845, more than 8,000 Americans were living in Oregon, most south of the Columbia River. Both the United States and Great Britain realized it was time to make an equitable division of the lands.

Pres. James K. Polk threatened war over the boundary early in his administration. His predecessor, John Tyler, and the British had been discussing the 49th parallel, the border between Minnesota and the Rocky Mountains. This was a compromise between the British desire to remain on the Columbia River and the Americans claiming it all to 54 degrees latitude, 40 degrees longitude on the map, or "54-40," today's Alaska. Polk at first resorted to jingoism to satisfy the Anglophobes in Congress, but the common sense of Secretary of State James Buchanan prevailed. By early 1846, the two nations agreed on the 49th parallel, as long as the United States possessed the Olympic Peninsula and Puget Sound. This was considered highway robbery by HBC chief factor James Douglas.

The treaty makers met in London in the spring of 1846 to hammer out the details. By the time what became known as the Oregon Treaty was signed in June, the boundary traced the 49th parallel and then ran south through the "channel" that divides Vancouver Island and the United States mainland. However, a problem remained.

The treaty makers presumed the channel, the Georgia Strait, ran unimpeded to the Strait of Juan de Fuca, totally discounting the San Juan Islands that block its path. The Americans thought the channel indicated in the treaty was the Haro Strait to the west. The British believed it was the Rosario Strait to the east. To maintain the peace, the nations agreed to hold the islands in dispute until the boundary was decided.

Also in 1846, the HBC's Fort Victoria had replaced Fort Vancouver as headquarters for company operations in the Pacific Northwest. Established in 1843 by Douglas on the southern tip of Vancouver Island, the "Fort" (as it was known) was the gathering place for British and American settlers and native peoples. They came to purchase supplies, swap news, make friends, sometimes settle scores, and later to catch steamers to San Francisco or up Puget Sound. Seven miles east across the Haro Strait, the San Juan Islands rose out of the sea like humpback whales—close enough for Douglas to consider the islands and all they possessed the rightful property of the HBC. On San Juan Island there were prairies for grazing sheep, timber to cut and dress, and five rich runs of salmon to be salted and barreled spring to fall. He vowed never to allow the Americans to barge in as they had along the Columbia.

But the Americans already were showing interest in real estate on Puget Sound, enough so that the resident populations of Coast Salish groups started to resist incursions into lands they had held for generations. The ensuing troubles brought the U.S. Army to the Oregon Territory not only to protect the Native Americans from U.S. settlers and vice versa, but also to keep tabs on the British Empire. Lucrative trade aside, the British army had burned Washington, D.C., only a generation before, and it was remembered in almost every household. The first U.S. units arrived on the banks of the Columbia in 1849 and established a post on the hillside overlooking the HBC's Fort Vancouver operations. The garrison was soon dispatching troops to address Native American unrest.

Meanwhile, the U.S. Coast Survey steamer *Active* first charted the San Juan Islands and the straits of Georgia and Juan de Fuca in 1853. In the process, the survey teams encountered the first rumblings of trouble over possession of the San Juan Islands. By now, the HBC held the government charter to the British Crown Colony of Vancouver Island, and Douglas was governor as well as chief factor. Hardly blinking at perceptions of conflict of interest, the governor since 1849 had been vigorously enforcing the company's proprietary rights over the land and resources of the islands. An American citizen attempting to harvest timber on neighboring Lopez Island complained to one survey crew that Douglas had warned him either to pay crown taxes or evacuate his claim.

Clearly pressures were building, and Douglas had served fair and early warning that he was not going to be shoved out of another region by the Americans.

One

"SETTLING"
SAN JUAN ISLAND

Hoping to further blunt American ambitions by, again, establishing prior claim and effective occupation on San Juan Island, James Douglas launched Belle Vue Sheep Farm on December 15, 1853, on prairie lands at the island's southern extremity. The site was named for the spectacular view of the Olympic Mountains rising over the Strait of Juan de Fuca.

The farm's initial inventory listed 1,369 sheep, one horse, one stallion, one mare, two cows and calves, one heifer, one boar, and one sow with young. Almost immediately, more pasture was sought and a road (which would one day link the military camps) was carved north to the center of the island to access San Juan Valley, then called Oak Prairie for its scatter of Garry oaks. Four other grazing areas were developed, each with a shepherd's hut and a log corral or "park." Charles John Griffin was selected to manage the operation, and he was good at his job. The flock expanded in six years to more than 4,500 head. In addition, he planted cereal crops, harvested timber, and salted and barreled fish caught by local Native Americans.

The farm drew immediate attention from Americans in the newly created Washington Territory, especially from the fledgling Whatcom County government, which sent a sheriff's posse to the island to impound 39 breeding rams for "back taxes." The international incident in the wake of this foolishness spurred the two nations to agree to a joint boundary survey from the Pacific Ocean to the Rocky Mountains. Her Britannic Majesty's Ship (HBMS) *Satellite*, the powerful steam corvette commanded by Capt. James Prevost, and the U.S. Coast Survey steamer *Active*, under Lt. Cmdr. James Alden, jointly plied the inland waterways and reached opposite conclusions about the water boundary. The British continued to believe the boundary was the Rosario Strait, the Americans the Haro Strait.

On the mainland, miners struck gold in 1858 up the Fraser River north of the 49th parallel. The strike heightened tensions because Americans from the California gold fields found British mineral rights laws repressive. These laws, combined with sparse yields, triggered a mass exodus within a year. Several miners drifted over to San Juan Island, lured by stories of cheap land for the taking just as soon as the boundary dispute was settled. It was only natural that they staked claims on the island's open prairies where there were no trees to cut down or stumps to pull.

George Edward Pickett was a newly minted second lieutenant in 1846, the year the Treaty of Oregon was signed. A native Virginian, Pickett received his West Point appointment from Illinois, where he had been sent to live with his maternal uncle with that object in mind. Thirteen years later, he would nearly drag his country into war with Great Britain over possession of the San Juan Islands.

Pres. James Knox Polk's rush in 1846 to gobble up lands west of the Rocky Mountains via the Treaty of Oregon and the Mexican-American War probably had a lot to do with the geographic sloppiness exhibited during the Anglo-American boundary negotiations. Polk served only one term, as he believed he had accomplished all he had set out to do. Shortly after his successor, Zachary Taylor, was inaugurated, he went home and died. (LOC.)

"WHAT? YOU YOUNG YANKEE-NOODLE, STRIKE YOUR
OWN FATHER!"

This popular political cartoon from the London newspaper *Punch* underscores the British attitude toward the United States at mid-19th century. Only 70 years after Lexington, Concord, and Bunker Hill, the precocious Yankees considered it their "Manifest Destiny" to lay claim to the entire continent. By April 1846, they had incurred the wrath of Mexico by annexing the Republic of Texas and by sending an army under Gen. Zachary Taylor to the border. A troop of Mexican dragoons rose to the bait and crossed the river to raid Taylor's camp, and Congress declared war in May. To make matters even more piquant, President Polk had declared "54-40 or Fight" over the Oregon boundary, sowing tension along the Columbia River. The British were alarmed enough to dispatch a warship to Fort Vancouver, 70-plus miles upriver. One British lord, in granting concessions on a Columbia River border, believed the move necessary in order to cultivate in the Americans "the arts of peace."

James Buchanan, the 15th president of the United States, was secretary of state in the Polk administration and was largely responsible for negotiating the Oregon Treaty with Great Britain in 1846. Only he and Sir John Pelly, a Hudson's Bay Company governor, raised alarms over the ambiguity in the Georgia Strait. Both were ignored. The lucrative economic relationship between the two nations was too compelling.

An antebellum 19th-century daguerreotype depicts Lt. Gen. Winfield Scott at the height of his power as commanding general of the U.S. Army. His Mexican War campaign was a set-piece example for cadets in both Europe and North America, but he was most celebrated as a peacemaker. He had already settled two border disputes with England before the Treaty of Oregon was signed. (LOC.)

The Royal Navy established its first permanent presence on Vancouver Island in 1855 when it erected what became known as the "Crimean Huts" in Esquimalt Harbor. The Hudson's Bay Company erected the buildings for the Royal Navy for use as a hospital to tend Crimean War wounded, but the war was over by the time they were completed. In 1860, the navy moved its Pacific Station headquarters to the site.

In 1853, James Douglas doubled as chief factor of the Hudson's Bay Company's (HBC) Fort Victoria and governor of the Crown Colony of Vancouver Island. He utilized the powers of both roles in establishing Belle Vue Sheep Farm on San Juan Island in December of that year. Not until early 1855 did the home government realize that the farm was an HBC entity and not a group of independent farmers.

Hudson's Bay Company (HBC) agent Charles John Griffin hides his workingman's fingernails as he poses for a Victoria photographer sometime in 1859. A native of Montreal, Griffin had been employed by the HBC for most of his working life, and the proprietorship of Belle Vue Sheep Farm was his first management opportunity.

Belle Vue Sheep Farm was the subject of a watercolor by Ensign James Madison Alden of the U.S. Coast Survey. The station was established on December 15, 1853, on the southern end of San Juan Island. Alden identifies the facility as belonging to the Puget Sound Agricultural Company, a subsidiary of the Hudson's Bay Company. But the station was established and administered by HBC officials on Vancouver Island, which is illustrative of its political importance to the British.

Two

THE PIG CRISIS

By spring 1859, a total of 18 Americans had settled claims staked on Hudson's Bay Company grazing lands, including a few parcels staked by surveyors on Oak Prairie. These they expected the U.S. government to recognize as valid, but to the British, the claims were illegal and the claimants little more than trespassers.

The crisis came on June 15, 1859, when Lyman Cutlar, one of the failed American miners, shot and killed a company pig rooting in his garden about a mile north of Belle Vue Sheep Farm. When British authorities threatened to arrest Cutlar and evict as trespassers all his countrymen from the island, a delegation sought military protection from Brig. Gen. William S. Harney, the anti-British commander of the U.S. Army Department of Oregon. Harney responded by ordering Company D, 9th U.S. Infantry, under Capt. George E. Pickett (of later Civil War fame) to San Juan. Pickett's 64-man unit—with two 12-pound mountain howitzers and one 6-pound Napoleon gun—landed on July 27 and encamped near the HBC wharf on Griffin Bay.

Governor Douglas quickly dispatched Capt. Geoffrey Phipps Hornby and the 31-gun steam frigate HBMS *Tribune* to dislodge Pickett but avoid an armed clash if possible. Hornby was soon joined by HBMS *Satellite* and HBMS *Plumper* with 21 and 10 guns respectively, plus 46 Royal Marines and 15 Royal Engineers. During his parley with Pickett, Hornby sensed that the U.S. government could not have sanctioned Pickett's landing. Consequently, when Pickett refused to budge, Hornby decided to ignore Douglas's orders and stand fast.

As July wore into August, Hornby accumulated more marines but held back until the arrival of Rear Adm. R. Lambert Baynes, commander of the British Pacific Station. An appalled Baynes told Douglas that he would not "involve two great nations in a war over a squabble about a pig."

On shore, Pickett was reinforced on August 10 by 171 men under Lt. Col. Silas Casey, who assumed command and by the end of August shifted the U.S. camp to the woods north of Belle Vue Sheep Farm. To solidify the United States' position, eight 32-pound naval guns were removed from the USS *Massachusetts* to be emplaced in a redoubt excavated under the direction of 2nd Lt. Henry M. Robert. While the Americans dug in, the British conducted drills with 62 (total) guns, alternately hurling solid shot into the bluffs along Griffin Bay.

By 1858, Victoria was a boomtown as well as the capital of the Crown Colony of Vancouver Island. The Hudson's Bay Company in 1849 had been awarded a royal grant to develop a colony around its trading post but had shown a reluctance to recruit settlers not employed by the company. All that changed when prospectors arrived from the Fraser gold fields.

This quieter, non-promotional photograph of Victoria was taken from the heights looking west down to the inner harbor. Note the flagpole, palisade, blockhouse, and barn-like structures of Fort Victoria at the center. Today's Fort Street in Victoria passes through the old parade ground to the wharf where the HBC steamers *Beaver* and *Otter* were tied. (LOC.)

The HBC established a fort, trading post, and coaling station at Nanaimo, about 60 miles north of Victoria on the east coast of Vancouver Island. It was the island's coal and heavy timber, as well as geopolitical expediency, that spurred the Royal Navy to move its Pacific Station headquarters there from Valparaiso, Chile. (BRBML.)

HBMS *Satellite* and the U.S. Coast Survey steamer *Active* are sketched at anchor in Bellingham Bay as part of the joint boundary survey undertaken by Britain and the United States in 1858. The *Satellite* also doubled as a police vessel, enforcing British laws among the miners. Bellingham Bay lies about 20 airline miles from Victoria and was the site of a transient miner's camp. (BRBML.)

James Douglas poses in his uniform around the height of the Pig War crisis. Douglas regarded his role as acting vice admiral seriously when the commander of the Royal Navy's Pacific Station was not at hand. It was largely considered an honorary title, but Douglas was accustomed to wielding power. He had blunted a takeover of lands that became British Columbia by using the Royal Navy to hold American miners in check. It was also Douglas who dispatched HBMS *Satellite* to San Juan Island to arrest Lyman Cutlar (the famous pig killer) and evict the 18 or so Americans occupying Hudson's Bay Company grazing lands. On hearing of the landing of U.S. Army troops under Capt. George Pickett, he next dispatched British warships to order Pickett off the island and use force if necessary.

Brig. Gen. William S. Harney (shown in the uniform of a major general) had a nasty reputation in the antebellum army. A well-connected Tennessean, he had received a direct commission at 18 from Pres. Andrew Jackson, which did not set well with West Point graduates. He relied heavily on Democratic Party patronage, especially when his commanding general, Winfield Scott, tried to have him court-martialed for insubordination. He had been sent to the Department of Oregon to fight Native Americans, but major fighting had ended by the time he arrived. He turned his nervous and irascible energy on the British. (LOC.)

Alexander Grant Dallas was a governor of the Hudson's Bay Company and one of the principal igniters of the Pig War crisis. It was Dallas who, along with two other company officials, threatened Lyman Cutlar on his doorstep. He then suggested in strong terms to Douglas that he arrest Cutlar and evict as trespassers all 18 Americans living on the island at the time. Dallas also was Douglas's son-in-law. (BCA.)

The officer who wrote Harney's orders to Pickett was Capt. Alfred Pleasonton, who was acting adjutant (administrative officer) for the department. He was a friend of George Pickett and went on to lead the Union cavalry corps at the Battle of Gettysburg. But he is best known among military historians for making 21-year-old George Custer a brigadier general. (LOC.)

Rufus Ingalls, shown as a brigadier general late in his career, was the acting quartermaster general at Vancouver Barracks in 1859, charged with supplying U.S. Army units throughout the department. He was George Pickett's closest friend and in 1865 warned him that he was being investigated for war crimes committed during the Civil War. Pickett named his favorite dog "Rufus" soon thereafter. (LOC.)

George E. Pickett poses in the uniform of a Confederate general, probably in 1863 at age 38. Only four years earlier, he had refused to decamp from San Juan Island while under the guns of three British warships. The opportunity to stand up to the British was beguiling, but being raked by more than 50 naval guns was not what he had in mind. (LOC.)

Pickett's first camp hugs the south shore of Griffin Bay (right center) while a longboat from HBMS *Satellite* heads for shore with the British magistrate aboard. The U.S. Lighthouse Tender *Shubrick* is anchored at left. A British midshipman aboard *Satellite* did the painting on July 27, 1859, the very day of Pickett's landing. Pickett had been ordered to encamp in a secure location, by which his superiors meant on the ridgeline out of range of British naval guns. He decamped from this position three days later, but pitched his tents on the opposite shore a half mile across the peninsula. The British were mystified. (BRBML.)

Pickett's second in command was 2nd Lt. James W. Forsyth, an able officer who made up for Pickett's poor engineering skills. The Maumee, Ohio, native was often left in charge by Pickett and not always in the most ideal conditions. It was Forsyth who endured a northeaster on San Juan in December 1859 and was then made accountable when the company gear was lost in a shipwreck. (LOC.)

Pickett's infantrymen came ashore garbed in the new dress uniform of the period: frock coat with shoulder scales and the new "Hardee hat," with one side of the brim turned up and garnished with an ostrich feather. The soldier in the photograph was actually a model whose visage is immortalized in the uniform of nearly every branch of the period. (NARA.)

Capt. James Prevost was not only in command of the 21-gun steam corvette HBMS *Satellite* when it steamed into Griffin Bay on July 27, he was also the British water boundary commissioner for the Northwest Boundary Survey. Imagine his surprise when, with no warning, he found Pickett's soldiers and artillery encamped on Griffin Bay. He accompanied British magistrate John DeCourcy to the U.S. camp to deal with the obstinate Virginian. (BCA.)

The deck of HBMS *Satellite* bristled with 8-inch guns, 10 on a side, plus a chase gun in the bow. Note the solid shot for the weapons at lower left. The ship's arrival in the Georgia Strait in 1858 effectively ended raids by Native American groups from the north. But *Satellite* was old-fashioned in one respect: Her guns could not be elevated to reach American guns eventually emplaced on the heights.

The British anchorage at Esquimalt Bay, just north of Victoria, provided an accessible and protected harbor good enough to establish a major foreign station for the Royal Navy. It was from here that *Satellite*, HBMS *Tribune*, and HBMS *Plumper* were dispatched to San Juan Island. The harbor remained a British base into the 20th century. (NARA.)

HBMS *Tribune*, a 31-gun steam frigate with a battle-seasoned crew, was sent to San Juan Island to threaten and intimidate Pickett in hopes that he would return to the mainland. *Tribune* epitomized the Royal Navy's mid-century transition from sail to steam, cruising under canvas at sea and steaming through inland waterways as she did in China during the Second Opium War. She was ideally suited for the San Juan Islands. (BCA.)

Capt. Geoffrey Phipps Hornby of HBMS *Tribune* was in his mid-30s and an officer on the rise in the Royal Navy at the time of the Pig War crisis. While it is true that his father, Phipps Hornby, was an Admiral of the Fleet, Geoffrey Hornby also had a special quality. On the *Tribune's* North Pacific crossing from Hong Kong to Vancouver Island in the winter of 1858, he almost single-handedly prevented the ship from foundering, at one point going aloft to secure a sail. Off San Juan Island, he refused, of his own volition, Douglas's orders to land Royal Marines because he considered the move provocative. These qualities ensured a future knighthood. His sense of humor is revealed in his letters home. He described George Pickett as sounding "almost like a Devonshire man." Hornby's son, Phipps Hornby, won the Victoria Cross in the Boer War. (Dr. William J. Schultz Collection.)

San Juan Village on Griffin Bay, the first permanent settlement on San Juan Island, sprang up only hours after Pickett established his camp on the opposite side of the lagoon. The "town" soon became, as Pickett described it, "a perfect bedlam day and night," home to prostitutes, murderers, whisky sellers, gamblers, sellers of bogus real estate, and all manner of thieves and scalawags. Most of the structures they occupied had been barged over from the abandoned miners' camp on Bellingham Bay. The respectable owners of the property turned a blind eye when there were dollars to be gained. The U.S. Coast Survey steamer *Active* is shown in the bay at right. HBMS *Satellite* is anchored off to the left. (BRBML.)

This alternate view of George Pickett in a Confederate officer's uniform, probably taken during an earlier session, shows him in better humor. But he was not smiling much in those late days of July 1859 when he rejected Hornby's offer of military parity on the island. One probably apocryphal pioneer account had him shouting, "We'll spike the guns and make a Bunker Hill of it!" (LOC.)

One of Pickett's first visitors after news of his landing swept Puget Sound was former territorial governor Isaac Stevens, soon to be departed for Washington, D.C., as territorial delegate to the U.S. Congress. Having been himself warned off from antagonizing the British over the San Juans, Stevens must have been relieved that Harney's act was on someone else's watch. (LOC.)

The complexion of the Pig War standoff changed profoundly when Rear Adm. R. Lambert Baynes arrived on August 5 in Victoria Harbor aboard his flagship HBMS *Ganges*, an 84-gun ship of the line. He had been an admiral since 1855 and in his current job since 1858. One Hudson's Bay Company official described him as "plain, little, big-hearted, unassuming, lowland Scotsman, lame but full of salt and fresh fun." However, Baynes took a dim view of the proceedings on San Juan Island. He immediately superseded Governor Douglas's orders to land Royal Marines and ordered Hornby to stand fast in the harbor and only fire if fired upon. "Tut, tut, no, no, the damned fools," he was heard to say on first hearing of the standoff. The queen knighted him the following year for maintaining the peace, which was the primary mission of the Royal Navy. (NAGB.)

The 84-gun HBMS *Ganges* was one of the last sailing ships of the line in the Royal Navy. As the name indicates, *Ganges* was built in Bombay, India, in 1820. *Ganges*'s role as Pacific Station flagship was her final commission, though she survived as a training ship well into the 20th century. No record exists of her anchoring off San Juan during the crisis.

Silas Casey poses in the uniform of a Union major general during the Civil War. The native Rhode Islander landed on San Juan on August 10 with 171 men and took command. His first act was to attempt a parley with the British in Victoria, but another standoff ensued when Baynes refused to disembark the mighty *Ganges* to wait on Casey aboard the U.S. Lighthouse Tender *Shubrick*. (LOC.)

Lt. Cmdr. James Alden was a naval officer attached to the U.S. Coast Survey who commanded the survey steamer *Active* on the West Coast for 10 years. A naval officer first and surveyor second, Alden warned Casey that the British might open fire if he attempted to land reinforcements. He carried dispatches from then on during the crisis. He was a direct descendant of John Alden and Priscilla Mullins of *Mayflower* fame.

Alden's friend and patron was Capt. David G. Farragut, who had been in command of Mare Island Naval Shipyard in San Francisco Bay, the *Active*'s homeport, in the mid-1850s. Alden became a superb blockade commander, serving almost exclusively under Farragut throughout the Civil War, from the Mississippi to Mobile Bay. (LOC.)

Henry Martyn Robert (shown as a West Point cadet) was a second lieutenant when he arrived on San Juan on August 21 to build a fortification. He selected a hillock overlooking both bay and strait and commenced his work, which alarmed Hornby. He enjoyed a long army career and penned *Robert's Rules of Order* after attending a stultifying church meeting.

Robert's redoubt was built to accommodate the eight naval guns from the deck of the USS *Massachusetts*. The guns had a range of about a mile and a half. The photograph above depicts a similar Civil War emplacement, although the guns are larger than the 32-pounders assigned to the *Massachusetts*. (LOC.)

In this illustration compiled from historical documents, the redoubt looms beyond the military camp on high ground commanding both Griffin Bay (left) and the Strait of Juan de Fuca. The excavation was regarded with alarm by the Royal Navy vessels anchored in the bay for two reasons: the guns' range (see page 32) and the fact that Hornby had been ordered not to allow the Americans to erect fortifications.

By the 1950s, Robert's redoubt was the most visible remnant of the Pig War crisis at American Camp, with its fully intact gun platforms and a monument erected in 1904 by the Washington State Historical Society. The structure has served as a triangulation point for the U.S. Coast Survey almost from the time of its construction.

Soldiers of Battery D, 3rd Artillery, pose with a Napoleon field gun sometime in October 1859 at the new permanent U.S. Army camp site selected by Lt. Col. Silas Casey. The soldiers wear the dress uniform prescribed in 1858, replete with ostrich plumes in their wide-brimmed hats. The soldier in the foreground is smoking what appears to be a corncob pipe. The National Park Service uses the same flagpole location today.

San Juan Island National Historical Park's collection includes a Napoleon gun nearly identical to the one pictured above. As indicated on the trunion, the gun was cast in 1836. The gun is on display at the Fort Lewis Military Museum in Tacoma, Washington.

Casey's second camp was relocated to the present site of the American Camp, just north of Belle Vue Sheep Farm, to better defend against a potential British assault. It also provided better shelter from storms that blow up the Strait of Juan de Fuca. The trees were eventually cut down to create fields of fire. The conical tents were designed by Maj. Henry Hopkins Sibley to emulate teepees.

This significant image of Belle Vue Sheep Farm shows it as it appeared in October 1859 at the height of the Pig War crisis. The image illustrates the classic Hudson's Bay Company (HBC) agricultural facility layout, with two rows of tidy log houses, heavy-duty fencing for sheep pens, and an English-style, double-bay barn in the background. Just beyond the barn was the permanent

U.S. Army camp established by Colonel Casey on August 21, 1859. The two gentlemen at far right are the British magistrate John DeCourcy (left) and Whatcom County sheriff Henry Crosbie (right). (BRBML.)

HBMS *Plumper* stands off while shore survey crews take hydrographic readings in Johnstone Strait along the northeast coast of Vancouver Island. *Plumper* was a steam sloop carrying at various times from 9 to 12 guns. At far right, a sailor takes a depth reading from the bow of a launch. The information was cross-checked from the towers erected by the crews ashore.

While the crisis mounted on San Juan Island, General Harney continued to apply pressure on the Hudson's Bay Company factory (above) on the Columbia River. Even then, the two governments were negotiating a settlement for the land and property. In this 1860 photograph, the joint Boundary Commission encamps on the parade ground before heading up the Columbia. (LOC.)

Three

AN INTERNATIONAL

INCIDENT

By mid-August, the so-called standoff had become great fun for the region's first tourists, who arrived on excursion boats from Victoria to tour the camp and be welcomed aboard the British ships. It was also a pleasant time for the officers of both sides, who attended church together and visited in HBC agent Charles Griffin's tidy house.

But when word reached Washington, D.C., officials from both nations, unaware of the bizarre atmosphere on San Juan, were shocked that Cutlar's pig murder had escalated into a potentially explosive international incident. The news had been sent east by courier to Washington by Harney on July 19 but did not arrive in the capitol from army headquarters in New York until September 3. In 1859, transcontinental mails were carried by ship through Panama or stagecoach cross-country from Carson City to Fort Leavenworth and thence by telegraph from St. Louis. Unfortunately, the British ambassador Lord Lyons read it first in the newspapers.

Lyons and U.S. secretary of state Lewis Cass exchanged notes that amplified with each new scrap of information and finally blew apart on September 13, when Royal Engineer Lt. Col. John S. Hawkins arrived from Victoria with a firsthand account. Lyons was so alarmed by Harney's posturing that he decided to forego the usual written dialogue and saw Cass in person. The two men agreed the situation called for a peacemaker on-site while the diplomats sorted out the larger questions at home. The obvious choice was Lt. Gen. Winfield Scott, the U.S. Army commander who had calmed two other northern border crises in Maine and New York in the late 1830s. Following a six-week passage via the Isthmus of Panama, Scott stopped first at the Vancouver Barracks on the Columbia River to assume temporary command of the Department of Oregon. He also took the opportunity to yank Harney and Pickett into his shipboard cabin to scold them for their "little conquest."

On his arrival in the San Juans in late October, Scott and Douglas arranged for each nation to withdraw reinforcements, leaving the island with a single company of U.S. soldiers and a British warship anchored in Griffin Bay. Scott proposed a joint military occupation until a final settlement could be reached, which both nations approved in November. Douglas was pleased to comply with a back-channel understanding that George Pickett and "his somewhat hasty temperament" would not command on San Juan Island.

President Buchanan's pained expression makes one wonder if the photograph was snapped shortly after hearing news of the Pig War crisis. In reality, Buchanan was in the unenviable position of being a lame-duck president while the country tore itself apart. Acting secretary of war William Drinkard wrote Harney, "The president was not prepared to learn that you had taken military possession of San Juan or Bellevue." Buchanan well remembered the flap Harney had caused over his court-martial during the Mexican war. At that time, the irascible Tennessean was James Polk's problem—now he belonged to Buchanan. (LOC.)

One way of sending word of the crisis to Washington City in 1859 was via overland stage from Carson City, Nevada, to the telegrapher at Fort Leavenworth, Kansas. The telegram went by steamer from Port Townsend to San Francisco, then up the Sacramento River and by horseback over the Sierra Nevada. The above image was possibly taken postwar because the soldiers are African American. (LOC.)

Fort Leavenworth, shown here in later years, was one of the jumping-off points in crossing the Great Plains by stagecoach or wagon train. Mark Twain lucidly described his journey on the overland stage to California in his book *Roughing It*. The post was also the westernmost telegraph station in the country in 1859. (LOC.)

Steamship travel was the preferred method of coast-to-coast travel before establishment of the transcontinental railroad in 1869. The journey involved catching a side-wheel steamer such as the one above to the Isthmus of Panama, then boarding a train for the 47-mile ride from Panama City to Aspinwall on the Atlantic side. From there, travelers caught another steamer to New York. The fare was $175. (LOC.)

The narrow-gauge Panama train chugged over the summit of the isthmus and down to the Caribbean in about two and a half hours. The steamship line promised that the northbound steamer would be ready to depart when the train pulled into Aspinwall, thereby guaranteeing limited exposure to the *vomito*, later known as yellow fever. (LOC.)

U.S. secretary of state Lewis Cass of Michigan (here striking the usual Napoleonic pose of the period) was given the task of convincing the British ambassador, Lord Lyons, that Harney's San Juan gaff was not sanctioned by the U.S. government. A native of New Hampshire and former frontier general, Cass was the Democratic Party's candidate for president in the 1848 election, which he lost to Zachary Taylor. (LOC.)

Richard Bickerton Pemell Lyons, First Viscount Lyons, was one of Britain's most able diplomats in the mid-19th century. As had Captain Hornby, Lyons rightly sensed that Harney had been acting on his own and thus made every effort to maintain the peace. He agreed that U.S. Army commander Lt. Gen. Winfield Scott was the best mediator available to send on the long journey west. (LOC.)

This remarkable 1860 Library of Congress image shows Lord Lyons, second from left, in a carriage in Portland, Maine, with the Prince of Wales (third from left), the Duke of Newcastle, and Mayor Howard of Portland. The anti-slavery Lyons was also instrumental in keeping the peace between the Union and Britain during the Civil War. (LOC.)

Capt. Charles Wilkes, who charted the San Juan Islands in 1841, ran afoul of Lord Lyons and the British in 1861 when he stopped the Royal Mail packet *Trent* on the high seas and removed two Confederate diplomats. This time, the British did not tolerate a slight that involved a disruption of commerce on the high seas. They threatened war if the Confederates were not immediately released. (LOC.)

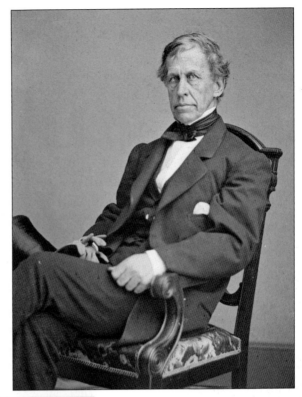

Winfield Scott was so aged, infirm, and obese on his trip west that he had to be derricked from ship to ship on the journey. By the time he reached the Strait of Juan de Fuca and transferred aboard USS *Massachusetts* (his flagship at Vera Cruz), he refused to leave his cabin and negotiated with Governor Douglas via messengers aboard revenue cutters. However, as a reporter for the *Daily Alta California* attested, he kept a "splendid table."

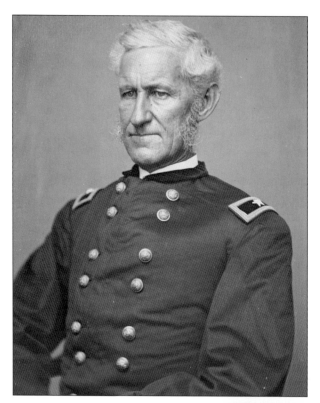

As Winfield Scott's chief of staff, Lt. Col. Lorenzo Thomas came west to run the general's headquarters as he had since 1853. He was appointed adjutant general of the U.S. Army in 1861 but was detailed out of Washington in 1862 after he attempted to declare then–brigadier general William S. Sherman insane. He retired in 1869. (LOC.)

After negotiating a stand-down, General Scott acceded to Governor Douglas's wishes by replacing Pickett (whom the governor detested) with Capt. Lewis Cass Hunt as commander of the first official U.S. joint occupation contingent. Hunt was fired a few months later after publishing several poison-pen letters about Harney, referring to him in one as a "retched stupid old goose." (LOC.)

Four

JOINT MILITARY OCCUPATION

When orders directing a joint military occupation reached Victoria in December 1859, the British selected for the site of their post a clearing on Garrison Bay, 13 miles north of the U.S. encampment. Thus English Camp was born on March 21, 1860, atop a midden of clamshells accumulated over 2,000 years of habitation by the Coast Salish people.

The Americans by then had settled into their camp. Eight companies or batteries from four regiments—all regular army—were eventually assigned under 15 different officers over the next 12 years. Through it all, the commanders took advantage of the Hudson's Bay Company sheep run, improving it into a military road that, before a telegraph was installed along its track in the mid-1860s, permitted rapid transit by horse and mule power. George Pickett preferred mules.

The route justified its expense when Harney replaced Hunt with Pickett in April 1860 and declared that he did not recognize the joint military occupation. Scott had never briefed him, he maintained, thus confirming Hunt's metaphor regarding his intelligence. But for the patience of Admiral Baynes, who accurately predicted Harney would be dumped by his government, the crisis could have reignited. This time, Pickett was a model of diplomacy and established with his counterpart, Royal Marine captain George Bazalgette, a precedent for friendship and cooperation between the two sides that continued over the years.

With the departure of Harney, the joint occupation quickly settled into 12 years of boredom for soldiers and marines, for both nations were committed to maintaining the peace. The only serious issues involved land disputes between respective nationals, which were quickly resolved by evictions, if necessary, and the seemingly never-ending pursuit of whiskey sellers and smugglers by joint patrols.

In May 1871, the British and Americans selected Kaiser Wilhelm I of Germany to settle the dispute via the Treaty of Washington. His three-man commission ruled two-to-one that the Haro Strait was the "southerly" channel dividing Vancouver Island from the mainland as cited in the Treaty of 1846. The San Juan Islands belonged to the United States. On Thursday, May 21, the Royal Marines abandoned their camp and returned to Vancouver Island. The Pig War was finally over.

The Royal Marine contingent landed on the site of an ancient Coast Salish habitation on today's Garrison Bay. They found ruins of a site very much like the one above located on Barkley Sound on Vancouver Island. Almost the entire saltwater estuary was covered by mounds of clamshells, which resembled, as one officer wrote, "drifts of snow." (BRBML.)

These forbearers of today's Lummi Nation considered Garrison Bay a sacred place and home to their ancestors going back thousands of years. Nearer to historic times, the village had become seasonal, with the occupants spending the winter and then moving on to other fishing and food-gathering grounds in the spring. (LOC.)

The Royal Marines, as this famous spring 1860 image affirms, went straight to work clearing brush, cutting trees, and constructing a fence to protect their vegetable garden from Columbia black-tail deer. The tents accommodated both the officers and enlisted men over the next several months. They also dismantled the ruins of a Native American house, located just beyond the fence.

As this August 1860 sketch by W. G. B. Willis attests, the enlisted men were still in tents while the officers were comfortably housed on the hill above. Admiral Baynes changed that after visiting the camp in late August. He requested building materials from Douglas and ordered the camp commander, Royal Marine captain George Bazalgette, to get cracking on housing the men before winter.

Capt. George Bazalgette (pronounced *Bazal-jet*) was Canadian-born and a 12-year Royal Marine veteran when he arrived on San Juan Island in 1860. He saw action in the Second Opium War in China in 1857 and was promoted to captain in 1858. He commanded the San Juan contingent for more than seven years, returning to England in August 1867.

This early-1860s view of Officers' Hill shows the officers' apartments on the lower terrace above the rock wall at lower left center. The marines constructed the walls by hand and filled them with earth and clamshells from the shell midden. Look carefully to spot a large birdhouse on a pole just to the right of the central structures.

In a detail from the photograph on pages 54–55, several Royal Marines pose in front of the noncommissioned officers' quarters probably around 1865. This group wears the globe insignia, topped by the light infantry badge (the "Bugle" or "hunter's horn"), on their Kilmarnock forage caps. The decorations worn by the middle marine indicate that he has served in a campaign(s), which also warranted a modest raise in pay.

This painting from the British Columbia archives is labeled "Roche Harbour, San Juan Island." The archives of three nations indicate that the camp never really had a formal name. It was known as the Royal Marine camp or Roche Harbour for the principal deepwater harbor in the area. For various reasons, islanders took to calling it the "English Camp" much later. The body of water is named for Lt. Richard Roche, RN. (BCA.)

This similar view to the painting above shows the camp at dead calm with mill-pond waters and the Union flag limp on the pole. The commissary or storehouse (with men gathered in front to the right of the sentry box) had double doors to facilitate launching of the camp longboat. It was built first to protect weapons and stores.

A sunny day on the parade ground is captured from the end of the steamer dock. Several marines are seated on the embankment, while another seems to be looking over a Native American canoe on the beach. The long building in the background is the main barracks. The blockhouse (or guardhouse) looms in the foreground.

British

An officer (perhaps Captain Bazalgette) poses with the San Juan contingent in front of the noncommissioned officers' quarters. The photograph can be identified as pre-1865 as the marines are wearing the Kilmarnock forage cap, which was soon to be replaced by the Glengarry. The photograph is also notable in that it reveals that a goodly portion of salt marsh still existed in the early years of the garrison. The land was soon drained and filled to serve as a new vegetable garden. Two of the men's heads are misshapen because they moved when the exposure was made.

55

While British officers in the Pacific Northwest were focusing on the joint occupation, Americans were looking east as the United States collapsed into civil war. There were promotions to win and glory aplenty in store, or so they thought. The realties were much grimmer for officers such as Brig. Gen. Isaac Stevens, who was mortally wounded at Chantilly in 1862. (LOC.)

Other officers such as Brig. Gen. Silas Casey found a safer course, though not necessarily by choice. Casey, shown here with his staff, had the misfortune of losing a fight for a redoubt against Confederate brigadier general George Pickett during the Battle of Seven Pines. He spent the remainder of the war training troops in Washington City and writing a book on infantry tactics. (LOC.)

Younger officers whose nascent antebellum service had shown promise saw their fortunes rapidly accelerate in a war that employed (and consumed) vast citizen armies requiring professional leadership. U.S. Army captain James W. Forsyth, seated second from left in this 1862 photograph, had already demonstrated his skill as an acting company commander on San Juan Island. Who could guess then that the self-confident fellow staff officer reclining at right would become the youngest brigadier general of the war? His name was George Custer. Their paths continued to cross after the war when Forsyth remained as a staff officer to Lt. Gen. Philip Sheridan. Forsyth was given command of the 7th Cavalry 10 years after Custer's death at the Little Bighorn and led the 7th at the so-called Battle of Wounded Knee in 1890. (LOC.)

BURNING OF THE U.S. SHIP OF THE LINE PENNSYLVANIA, 140 GUNS.
and other Vessels, at the Gosport Navy Yard, Norfolk Va on the night of April 20th 1861.

In April 1861, Secretary of the Navy Gideon Welles ordered Cmdr. James Alden to Norfolk, Virginia, to remove USS *Merrimack* before the rebels captured the naval yard. But Alden would not overrule the yard commander and, to Welles's disgust, returned to Washington without the ship. *Merrimack* was scuttled and soon resurrected as the CSS *Virginia*, the Confederacy's first ironclad warship. (NOAA.)

Brig. Gen. Alfred Pleasonton, shown here with then-1st lieutenant George Custer, became the first commander of the unified Union cavalry corps. Pleasonton was banished west after his leadership was found wanting at Gettysburg, though some believed it was because he shouted at Meade: "Go after them, you damn fool!" when Pickett's men fell back. Custer quickly shifted his allegiance to Pleasonton's replacement, Lt. Gen. Phil Sheridan.

It was on July 3, 1863, that Pleasonton and George Pickett converged at the crossroads town of Gettysburg, Pennsylvania. Here Pickett doffs his cap to Lt. Gen. James Longstreet prior to attacking the center of the Union line on the battle's third day. Pleasonton's cavalry, led by Custer among others, foiled Maj. Gen. Jeb Stuart's attack on the Union rear. The action was known then as "Longstreet's Second Assault."

Pickett's Charge involved only three of Pickett's brigades out of the 11 that crossed the field that day. But Pickett's division suffered 2,655 casualties out of 5,848 men (498 killed, 643 wounded, 833 wounded and captured, and 681 captured unwounded). Pickett never recovered from the trauma of the slaughter and blamed Gen. Robert E. Lee. No matter, Col. John Mosby, the "Gray Ghost," told him years later, "it made you immortal."

That James Alden was a direct descendant of John Alden and Priscilla Mullins of *Mayflower* fame and a skilled ship handler probably preserved him from career harm following the *Merrimack* debacle. His Coast Survey skills served him well in blockade duty, and he rose to become captain of the powerful steam sloop USS *Brooklyn* and one of Admiral Farragut's trusted lieutenants. (LOC.)

It was Capt. James Alden and the USS *Brooklyn* that led the Union line into Mobile Bay under Fort Morgan's blazing guns in 1864. When the monitor USS *Tecumseh* capsized after striking a mine, Alden reversed course and the *Brooklyn* drifted abeam into the oncoming line, jeopardizing the attack. It was then that Farragut shouted, "Damn the torpedoes," and the flagship USS *Hartford* steamed past *Brooklyn* and into legend.

Back on San Juan Island, the Royal Marine camp welcomed a new commanding officer in June 1867, Capt. William Addis Delacombe, who brought his family from England. Here they pose on the steps of the commander officer's house, which was sited on the topmost terrace on Officers' Hill. The officer at far left appears to be Lt. Herbert S. G. Schomberg, who did not arrive at the camp until 1871. (LOC.)

Here is another view of the same photo session, only this time, Delacombe includes his horse. From the start, the British preferred traveling the Military Road by horseback. The Americans opted for mules, except for in horse racing, in the early days. Once Captain Pickett was thrown by his horse during a race at American Camp. According to witnesses, Pickett's men doffed their hats and cheered.

This shot shows the Delacombes and the house again in earlier days. Note that the ivy was much fuller and that the porch is fitted with what appears to be adjustable awnings, probably fashioned of canvas. The fact that there is no baby in the photograph probably indicates that the photograph was taken shortly after the Delacombes arrived in the late 1860s.

This shot of the commander's house, sans family, reveals one of the family's favorite activities: tennis. The enlisted men constructed the court by extending the rock wall and filling the entire area with clamshells from the parade ground and earth from other, less rocky areas of the camp. The terrace still exists.

Captain Delacombe (far left) takes his ease on the junior officers' terrace with (from left to right) August Hoffmeister, the camp storekeeper; Royal Navy surgeons Thomas Redfern and Robert Potter; Delacombe's son, Willie; and the family dogs, Tommy and Erouda. These are the structures shown on page 51. The bachelor officers' quarters are to Delacombe's left. The camp surgeon used the house at right.

This view of the commander's house is a puzzle. Past National Park Service historians believed that the house is shown recently completed in 1867. Note that the front steps are sans end posts and the decorative spandrels are missing. This photograph also could have been taken after the house was renovated in 1893.

The U.S. Army camp appears complete in this view taken in 1868. The buildings at right center beyond the fence formed the hospital complex, the barn is at left center, and the barracks/cookhouse complex is at far right. Officers' row is at far left with the two-story structure assigned to the commanding officer. The house at far left still stands where the parade ground was once defined and is preserved by the National Park Service. Strong evidence exists that the adjoining quarters is located at West and First Streets in Friday Harbor and that the commander's house is a family residence, also in Friday Harbor. The buildings were auctioned in 1875, one year after the camp was abandoned. The government made more than $1,300 from the sales.

Camp San Juan Island

A folk painting, probably from the same era as the photograph at left, allows the viewer to perceive the camp in motion, something mid-19th-century photographs could not capture. Here we see the soldiers at drill, a wagon unloading behind the cookhouse, and the busy spur of Military Road leading to the Griffin Bay landing.

The American Camp hospital ward is shown in the late 19th century after it had been converted to a barn with structures added on either end. This same structure with its ventilated roof can be identified at right center in the photograph at left. The building did not collapse until the mid-1960s.

This splendid view of the blockhouse, barracks, and Union flag at full flight at the Royal Marine camp was probably taken around 1865. The shops, reading room, and carpenter's shop have yet to be added on the hill above the barracks.

Former HBC employee Angus McDonald caused a flap in the late 1860s when he sublet an American-owned farm five miles south of English Camp to another British subject. Delacombe forcibly evicted the British man, who had worked the land for two years in the owner's absence. The act underscores the importance both nations placed on maintaining the peace. (BRBML.)

Shortly after his arrival, Captain Delacombe planted the garden above for his wife to remind her of home. The National Park Service reconstructed the garden in 1972 and over the years has interpreted it as a "Formal Garden." But Mrs. Delacombe identified the plot merely as a "strawberry garden" in the margin of the original photograph. The ship at the dock is HBMS *Boxer*.

These engravings (probably taken from photographs) were created to illustrate news and feature stories concerning the two camps. They are labeled "early 1870s" in the park archives. In the Royal Marine camp view, note the commander's house (including a carriage house to the left) standing tall on Officers' Hill. American Camp is more simplistically rendered, although by the late 1860s the camp was falling apart. The barracks was in such poor condition that men were sleeping in the barn (top center). The U.S. Congress did not appropriate $1 to maintain the camp throughout its existence.

This heretofore-unknown view of the bachelor officers' terrace was taken a few years later than the image on page 63. Note that the surgeon's house has been expanded, the younger trees have grown, and a gate has been installed to the rear of the structures. From left to right are Delacombe, August Hoffmeister, Dr. and Mrs. Alexander Allen, and Lieutenant Schomberg (also pictured on page 61). (Delacombe family.)

This splendid c. 1870 view of Officers' Hill gives some indication of the size of the commanding officer's and married subaltern's houses in relation to the other buildings in the camp, including the other commissioned officers. Note the bachelor officers' quarters on the lower terrace and the longboat in the boat shed on the beach below. (Delacombe family.)

This panorama from the Delacombe family album, still held by direct descendants in England, is the only known image to present a relatively complete view of the camp just before the end of the joint occupation. By then, the physical plant included several outbuildings adjacent to the commanding officer's house. These included the stables and carriage house (see page 88). It is also possible to see all four buildings on the hill above the barracks where several marines are congregating, probably in full knowledge that their picture is being taken. The bay is at flood tide and enveloping the base of the blockhouse. Delacombe's great-grandson, visiting from England in 2006, brought along a CD that included this photograph as well as those on pages 69–73. While a few of these photographs appear in several collections in the United States, England, and Canada, this and several others have never been made public. (Delacombe family.)

Families from Victoria and those of the English Camp officers gather under the bigleaf maple near Mrs. Delacombe's strawberry garden during the visit of the admiral from Royal Navy headquarters at Esquimalt Harbour. Mrs. Delacombe is second from left, and her son Willie is the blur (he moved) second from right. Note the officers standing on the parade ground beyond. (Delacombe family.)

Mrs. Delacombe, her friends, and children are now sitting at lower right to watch Adm. A. Farquhar, just left of center with stripes on his sleeve, review the troops in the early 1870s. Delacombe, wearing a shako hat, snaps a left-handed salute, his sword in his right hand. The marines are in full dress with white cross belts as befitting the occasion. (Delacombe family.)

In another panorama, taken from what Mrs. Delacombe called "The Point," the camp is not only tidy but also impressive in size. The viewer is, again, able to grasp the sheer size of the officers' structures, even though they are in the background. This underscores the fact that as with most military camps, no matter the country, the officers and enlisted men lived in two separate worlds—even so far from home. (Delacombe family.)

Royal Marines drift onto the beach at Guss Island, perhaps to do some clam digging, in this *c.* 1868 view showing the camp in the background. This vessel is likely the one viewed in the boat shed adjoining the shipping dock. The National Park Service protects Guss Island as a cultural site; it is closed to the public. (Delacombe family.)

The Delacombe album also contained this image of the commanding officer's house at American Camp. It is the only known close-up of one of the U.S. buildings during the life of the camp and is unique in that it shows British and American officers and their families gathered on the porch. The little girl at far left sits on a push-along tricycle fashioned to be a pony. (Delacombe family.)

The Royal Marine parade ground is shown as it appeared prior to the extension of the privates' mess as a barracks (see map, page 76). The diminutive size of the marines sitting on the porch of the main barracks should give the viewer some idea of its mass. The photograph was probably taken from the steamship dock near the strawberry garden. (Delacombe family.)

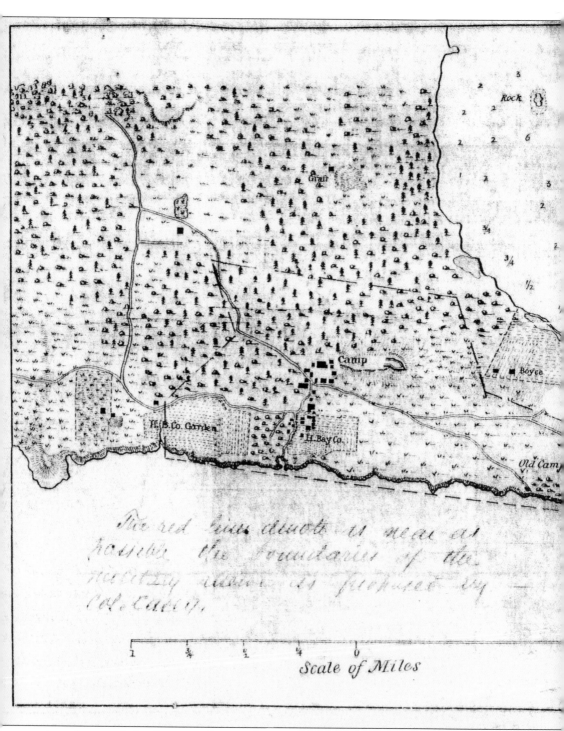

Rock

Graft

Camp

Boyce

H. B. Co. Garden

H. Bay Co.

Old Cam

The red lines denote as near as
possible the boundaries of the
military reserve as furnished by
Col. Casey.

1   ¾   ½   ¼   0

Scale of Miles

As early as 1860, the American Camp military reservation encompassed the entire Cattle Point Peninsula save for San Juan Village and environs. Captains Pickett and Bazalgette took action to redraw their respective boundaries after a Royal Marine contingent caught some Americans excavating lime at the site of today's Roche Harbor Resort. In turn, Bazalgette's camp boundary

*Tracing
From a map of the
South-east end of
San Juan Island
Prepared by
Lieut. James W. Forsyth ...
Date and sources not stated.*

*Official:
Louis V. Caziarc
1st Lt. 2d Arty
A.A.I.*

*Dept. Columbia
Portland Oregon
Nov. 4, 1872*

HARBOR

Wharf

Fishing Station

Hibbs

Channel

Rock

Rock

*The original of this
map accompanies
Letter (P27) Department
of the Columbia Record
for the Dist. of Oregon
1860. Filed in A.A.G.O.*

dominated the northern end of the island. Pickett's boundary was a time bomb that went off when an American farmer erected a fence barring the army from the old HBC dock. The army evicted him from the island, which did not sit well with civilians.

The Royal Marine contingent poses in formation on the parade ground around 1872. The men are now wearing the navy-blue Glengarry cap. By then, the camp boasted new shops, a library, and sergeants' mess room situated on the hill above the barracks. The former privates' mess room (right) has been extended into a barracks.

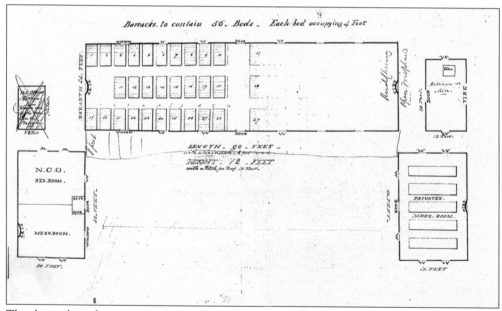

The above plans, drawn in 1860 by Royal Engineers captain Robert Parsons, show the main barracks with the noncommissioned officers' quarters, cookhouse, and privates' mess room. Parsons had to do the work in civilian clothes, as the camps were limited to 100 military personnel each. Guns (cannons) were prohibited as part of the joint military occupation agreement. (NAGB.)

Among the notable American Civil War Union officers to serve as Department of the Pacific commanders (headquartered in San Francisco) during the joint occupation were Irvin McDowell and Henry W. Halleck, both major generals. McDowell (right) came west in 1864 in time to declare that military rule would continue on the island, thus drawing the ire of civil authorities in Washington Territory. Halleck arrived in 1867 and pronounced that the entire territory should be placed under martial law and be done with it. He next endeared himself to the British by declaring that they were too flaccid a race to colonize British Columbia. (LOC.)

By January 1870, Great Britain and the United States agreed to the formation of a joint high commission to resolve a number of disputes between them, including the San Juan boundary. The British commission above is, from left to right, (seated) Sir Stafford Northcote, Earl De Grey and Ripon, and Sir Edward Thornton; (standing) Lord Tenterden, Canadian prime minister Sir John A. MacDonald, and Montague Bernard. The American commission included Robert Schenck, Ebenezer Hoard, Secretary of State Hamilton Fish, George Williams, Samuel Nelson, and Bancroft Davis.

Canadian prime minister Sir John MacDonald was the first to hold that office in the new Dominion of Canada (1867) and remained in power for more than 19 years. He was instrumental in making Canada a continental nation by bringing British Columbia into the dominion in 1871, when the San Juan question was under binding arbitration.

Secretary of State Hamilton Fish was Pres. Ulysses S. Grant's longest-serving cabinet officer and a tough negotiator. When one of the German adjudicators suggested including the narrow Middle Channel that divides the islands, Fish insisted that the decision be between the Haro and Rosario Straits or the United States would withdraw. The British, wanting to be done with the San Juans, went along with Fish.

Both nations agreed that Emperor William (Kaiser Wilhelm I) of the newly constituted German Empire should be arbiter of the San Juan dispute. George Bancroft, the U.S. ambassador in Berlin, recommended him. The Kaiser appointed a three-man commission who convened in Geneva for a year before ruling that the San Juans belonged to the United States.

U.S. Army brigadier general Edward Canby (shown as a major general during the war) was commander of the Division of Oregon by 1872. He apologized that no guns were available to fire a farewell salute to the Royal Marines, as artillery was prohibited during the joint occupation. Canby was killed the following year while parleying with the Modoc Indians in northern California. He was the only general killed in the Indian Wars.

The Camp San Juan Island commander, 1st Lt. James Haughey, rode to Garrison Bay to say farewell to the British. A few days later, he dispatched a contingent under his second in command, 2nd Lt. Fred Epstein, to guard and survey the camp. They took along a giant flag to run up the British pole but soon discovered it had been chopped down. The British claimed they had salvaged the pole for the Esquimalt naval base.

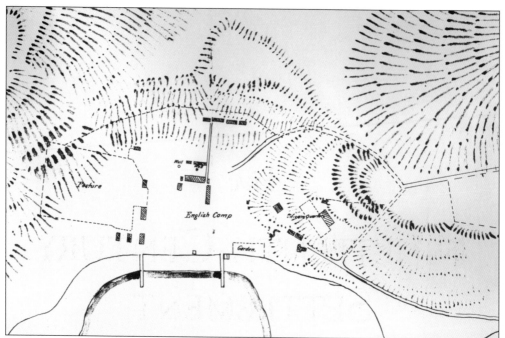

In 1874, U.S. Army major Nathaniel Michler completed the most accurate map known of English Camp (above) as a follow-up to Ebstein's inventory. Two years later, William Crook, a British immigrant, claimed English Camp and its surrounding reservation and filed a claim for the land under the Homestead Act of 1862.

According to Crook's daughter, Rhoda Crook Anderson, the Royal Marine camp was largely intact and in good condition when they moved on-site. The family was living there when the U.S. government auctioned the buildings. The former shop and library on the hill overlooking the parade ground number among the 15 structures (of 27 total) that remained in the Crooks' possession. The brick edifice has been identified as the ruins of a combination forge and bake oven, although this remains open to debate.

Five

NINETEENTH-CENTURY SETTLEMENT

San Juan Island was an ideal place to settle during the joint military occupation largely because of the well-armed companies of Royal Marines and U.S. soldiers. Pioneer settlers, mainly farmers, also fondly recalled that because of the islands' disputed status, no property or related taxes had to be paid.

The 1870 census listed 184 male residents of the archipelago, 96 on San Juan Island. Of the 46 British subjects, more than half remained to become U.S. citizens, and some descendants live on the island today. By 1874, the island had been surveyed and formal claims were being filed under the Homestead Act of 1862. The claims included one in 1876 by William Crook, a British immigrant who had settled on the Royal Marine campsite the year before with his wife and two children.

At American Camp, parcels identified belonged to Robert Firth (the last Hudson's Bay Company agent), Joseph Sandwith Jr., Thomas J. Weekes (a Presbyterian minister), Henry Webber, Christopher Rosler, William Taylor, and Robert H. Frazer. The Firths occupied the former officers' quarters, which still stands and has been restored to original configuration by the National Park Service.

Another American Camp claimant was George Jakle, who with his wife, Liza, occupied all the lands that today compose the park's Jakle's Lagoon/Mount Finlayson trail network. Jakle was Liza's second husband. The first, Henry Bryant, was a former army private from the camp who had purchased the claim from the deputy collector of customs, Paul K. Hubbs. When Bryant drowned in the lagoon, Liza soon took up with Jakle, also a former American Camp soldier. The couple contended with the U.S. government over possession of their land until the 1920s.

Many of these early settlers lived in buildings auctioned off by the U.S. Army in November 1875. The stipulation was that the buildings had to be removed from the premises within 60 days or they became the property of the land claimant. For the most part, this process went smoothly, with the exception of the opulent commander's house at English Camp. William Crook contended that, by auction rules, the house belonged to him and not Maj. E. W. Blake, who claimed that he and Crook had an "understanding." Ownership was tied up in the courts until 1879, when the Crooks became full owners. The building burned to the ground in 1894.

The William Crook family climbs into the bigleaf maple tree that still stands adjoining the surviving Royal Marine barracks. It is presumed that the bearded patriarch at center is William Crook and the woman to his left is his wife, Mary Crook. His eldest daughter, Mary Crook Davis, is at right in the foreground. The tree still tempts climbers of all ages, which the National Park Service tries to discourage with a split-rail fence.

An unidentified woman plumbs the well/cistern located near the surviving Royal Marine barracks. The Crooks lived in the building over the years between stretches in the commander's and subaltern's residences. The wells were excavated by the Royal Marines early in the camp's history and were used by the National Park Service to irrigate the formal garden until the late 1990s.

The Crooks developed an orchard, shown here around 1900, on the former Royal Marine parade ground. San Juan Island was famous for cultivation of fruit until the development of the industry in central Washington. Several of these trees still exist on the parade ground, along with another (older) orchard in the park on the slopes of Young Hill. Note the giant, bigleaf maple at right, which at one time was the largest of its species in the world.

Another view of the Crook orchard and the Royal Marine blockhouse shows more of Garrison Bay's unoccupied far shoreline, today a haven for vacation homes and permanent residences. This image can be viewed in contrast with the photograph shown on page 67. The two piles of rock poking out of the water at left center are all that is left of the original dock.

The Crook estate still looked like a military camp in 1880. The commander's house is located in the trees at upper right. The buildings on the terrace, left center, have been identified as the company mess and carpentry shop. The library has been torn down. Note that the blockhouse and commissary, two of the oldest buildings on-site, are still in pretty good shape.

The commander's house is gone in this flood-tide view, which dates it as post-1894. The rectangular masonry ruin, better known as the "forge," is visible at far center left. There has been some logging activity, and one of the buildings adjacent to the commissary has been torn down and another added.

In this post-1903 view, the Crooks' new house has been built immediately adjacent to the forge ruins at far left and the Royal Marine mess room and shops are gone. As in the two previous views, Young Hill, with its bald south face, looms in the background. Striations from the ancient Fraser glacier remain visible on its summit as evidence that a mile of ice once covered the entire island.

This 1890s close-up of the blockhouse, also taken at flood tide, reveals that a door has been cut on the waterside of the log base. The overgrown fruit orchard crowds the shoreline, much as native species must have when the Royal Marines arrived in 1860. Steps to Officers' Hill zigzag up the bluff (center right) above the crumbling remains of the boat shed.

The commanding officer's stables still stood on Officers' Hill when this undated image was taken. The rock walls were erected almost entirely by hand and filled with earth and clamshells by the enlisted men. The stables housed a carriage in addition to horses.

"The Old Broadway" road and/or path once led to the parade ground at the Royal Marine camp. The marines built the fence at right to delineate the camp cantonment area, much as the white picket fence was used at American Camp.

A family enjoys a picnic at the Crook Farm at English Camp around 1900. The well/cistern at left indicates that the table was set up on the fringe of the parade ground, probably at the foot of the hill where the Crook home stands today. The Crooks welcomed sightseers throughout their long ownership of the property, at times for a modest fee.

Another family explores the blockhouse, which has undergone some haphazard repairs. The original logs are bared at upper left, and the roof over the porch has been reduced to frame timbers. The National Park Service today renovates the blockhouse and remaining structures on a regular schedule.

After living alternately in several Royal Marine structures over the years, the Crooks built their own house on the hill overlooking Garrison Bay in 1903. The man sitting in the center on the porch is Jim Crook. The Crook house has been unoccupied since Rhoda Crook Anderson's death in 1972.

At American Camp, officers' row maintained its basic shape throughout the late 19th century. The two-story commanding officers' house was eventually moved to Argyle, a tiny village (now a neighborhood) farther north on Griffin Bay, while the bachelor officers' duplex in the foreground remained as the Firth family home.

The bachelor officers' quarters were still in use as a residence during the Firth era. This southwest-corner view indicates that the porch continued to encompass three sides of the structure and that the exterior door led to the kitchen of the farmhouse. The McRae family removed the extensions after they purchased the property in the early 1920s.

From the southeast, the Firth-era officers' quarters is looking a bit rundown but still retains some of the features George Pickett had known during his time at the post in the early 1860s. The telescoping additions (running downhill) that appeared in an 1876 map of the post are evident.

Turkeys and geese feed where soldiers once marched in this dawn-of-the-20th-century view of the Firth farm. The building is presumably one of the laundress quarters that housed a soldier, his wife, and children. One of Pickett's laundresses, Catherine McGarry, spent the rest of her long life on the island, acquiring considerable real estate and a comfortable income. She is buried in the island's Catholic cemetery.

With an assist from a newfangled steam engine, the Firths, neighbors, and hired hands take in the late summer hay harvest on the Jakle place looking south toward the Strait of Juan de Fuca in this 19th-century view. For years, this photograph has been mistakenly associated with the old parade ground. The Jakle house clearly appears in the background left. Over the crest of the hill is South Beach.

Sometime after the McRae family acquired American Camp from the Firths, they changed the orientation of the house's (top center right) front porch from north, facing the parade ground, to south for the view of the Strait of Juan de Fuca and Olympic Mountains. The family poses with their automobile in their potato field. Note the well tower to the right of the house.

This closer and earlier view of the same scene (sans well tower) offers a better view of the house, fencing, and outbuildings. The other house at far left is a newer structure, erected after the old commanding officer's house had been moved to Argyle. When the national park was established in 1966, this house was moved.

Belle Vue Sheep Farm's HBC-style cabins and outbuildings survived into the 20th century, albeit in a dilapidated state. This view is facing south toward the Strait of Juan de Fuca. Compare this view with one on pages 14 and 36–37.

The ruins of the American Camp cemetery gate and some of the fencing also endured into the 20th century. The human remains were moved to Fort Townsend after 1874. Much has been made of the fact that two sergeants committed suicide during the life of the camp. It was, in fact, a small percentage of those who served. Plus, it was not unusual on frontier outposts, where drink and boredom took their toll.

For years, the only indication that the landscape on the Cattle Point Peninsula had been an army post was the nearly perfectly preserved redoubt. In 1904, the Washington State Historical Society erected a monument that acknowledged George Pickett and the first encampment, as well as the Kaiser's decision. The National Park Service moved the monument to the visitor center parking area in the 1990s to save it from vandals.

Henry Martyn Robert rose to become a brigadier general and was appointed chief of engineers of the U.S. Army Corps of Engineers in 1901. But as mentioned earlier (page 32), he is more famous for writing *Robert's Rules of Order*, still the leading manual of parliamentary procedure in the world. His great-granddaughter lives near American Camp.

Jim Crook (shown seated forward) and another man strike out in a longboat from his dock on Garrison Bay. The shoreline at upper right is fenced along the bluff and then to the waterline, which may delineate a property line. The boat engine is located amidships along with a small fuel tank. Crook was an enthusiastic inventor whose outbuildings were full of machinery, including his own wool-carding machine.

American Camp's first post sutler and ubiquitous Washington pioneer, Ed Warbass came to San Juan Island in 1859 with George Pickett and lived on the island off and on until his death in 1906. Warbass claimed that the house above was Pickett's quarters, but the building was actually one of the laundress quarters. The house was moved to the park and returned to its original configuration in 1972. Note the inset in the photograph, believed to be Warbass and his dog.

This close-up view of the past and future laundress quarters features Edward Warbass himself in his rocking chair looking up from his newspaper. Warbass supported his claim that the house was once George E. Pickett's quarters by hanging a painting of Pickett in Confederate livery over his fireplace. The National Park Service returned the house to its original configuration by cutting off the late-19th-century addition about where the porch ends at left rear.

Six

LEGACY
THE CAMPS IN THE MODERN ERA

By the mid-20th century, it became apparent to many on the island that life, as they had known it, was changing irrevocably. The extraction industries of logging, fishing, and farming that had fueled the island's economy since the establishment of Belle Vue Sheep Farm in 1853 were dwindling to the point that a standard 160-acre quarter section was no longer enough to sustain a single family.

The network of reclamation projects along the Columbia River, and the glut of fruit and other agricultural produce they spawned, spelled the end of island orchards as a life-sustaining enterprise. Much as today's islanders, Crook and his counterparts, the McRaes, and subsequent landholders at American Camp developed multiple means to sustain their households. Crook raised sheep for wool and meat, cut hay, and was a skilled boatbuilder and barrel maker. Into his 80s, Crook developed severe arthritis, which forced him to walk with two canes. Eventually, his aged and widowed sisters, Mary and Rhoda, alternately returned to the farm to assist him.

The farm continued to be an attraction for tourists by land and water, who were charged a modest fee to poke around the grounds. In 1963, the Crooks transferred ownership of the parade ground proper to the Washington State Recreation Commission. By September 1966, largely through the efforts of U.S. senators Henry M. Jackson and Warren Magnuson and U.S. representative Lloyd Meeds (all D-Washington), San Juan Island National Historical Park was established with an allocation of more than $3 million to purchase properties that encompassed both military reservations.

Assembling American Camp was more of a challenge than English Camp as the site involved acquiring more than 1,200 acres of prime real estate already slated for development into a vacation resort. Fortunately, the owners were farsighted enough to understand that, coupled with its national significance, the site's natural prairie, forests, and saltwater shoreline were worthy of preservation for all Americans—most especially the islanders.

Today the National Park Service combines the sciences of cultural and natural history to tell the inseparable stories of land and people and celebrates a war where the only casualty was a pig.

Jim Crook poses with his dog and automobile at the blockhouse, which appears to be in the same condition as in the photograph on page 90, with the exception of the knocked out loopholes in the top story. Note the fence in the background. The National Park Service has erected similar fencing to protect the embankment and its cultural resources from further erosion. The shoreline across the bay is still unoccupied in this image.

The interior of the upper floor of the blockhouse, coated with lime-based whitewash, is almost entirely original to this day, thanks to Crook's modest efforts at historic preservation. The loopholes were designed for riflemen to repel attackers, although in reality, they provided the only illumination for miscreant marines serving time for drunkenness or taking "French leave" (desertion).

The Royal Marine cemetery was established on the slopes of Young Hill with the first marine death in 1863. After 1872, the cemetery was tended inconsistently, at least judging from 1903 and 1930 letters critical of its condition posted to the *Globe and Laurel*, the Royal Marines periodical. Crook maintained that the British government paid him a $10 monthly stipend for its care.

Jim Crook (fifth from left) joins members of the Royal Canadian Navy, who rededicated the cemetery in 1962 after researching the graves and making repairs twice in the late 1950s. A British Royal Navy study in 1903 was able to match names and graves (see page 102), although no one was able to catch the misspelling of one marine's name until 2004.

English Camp *near* Roche Harbour
San Juan Island U.S.A.

Sketch shewing Graves of Marines on land belonging to V. J. Capron Esq. M. D. of Roche Harbour.

Number of Mound	Name	Rank	Death Date	Death Cause	Age Years	Description of Head Stone
1	Unknown					
2	Charles Wood	Private	Jany 8th 1869		28	Stone Tablet
2	James Wensley	Dt	April 7th 1869	Drowned Accidentally		
3	William Taylor	Dt	Jany 26th 1868	shot by brother	34	Dt
4	William Davis	Dt	May 7th 1864	Drowned	26	Dt
5	Jos. Ellis	Dt	Jany 4th 1865	Drowned		Dt
5	Thos. Riddy					
6	Unknown					
7	G. E. Stewart	Corporal	June 1st 1863		31	Wooden Cross

Scale 1 In - 8 Ft

No. 503
1 DEC. 1903
ESQUIMALT

N. S. H. Q.
65385
CURATOR'S NUMBER

Civil Engineer
1·12·03.

This chart from the Royal Navy's 1903 cemetery study was done in response to the critical letter in the *Globe and Laurel*. It indicates seven graves and nine occupants, and of these, only six are identified as Royal Marines. One body was never found, so only five marines are buried on-site. One name is misspelled, according to Royal Marine records: Thomas Riddy should read Thomas Kiddy. Rest in peace, Thomas.

The Royal Marine cemetery has been well maintained after the National Park Service acquired the site in 1966. All four masonry headstones are original. Note the globe and laurel symbol of the Royal Marines on the stones at far right and third from right. Union flags appear on the graves on Queen Victoria's birthday each May.

Fishers began exploiting the annual salmon runs off South Beach more than 2,500 years ago, but the biggest takes occurred when commercial fish traps were introduced to the region in the 1880s. In principle, the technique was similar to reef netting, the timeless Native American method that trapped fish by means of a false reef fashioned of cedar rope and anchored to the sea floor with rocks. The commercial traps (above) were more capital-intensive, involving the creation of net barriers or "leads" affixed to piles and running up to 400 yards long. Migrating fish encountered the leads and then swam along them into the "hearts," a series of inverted "Vs" that forced the fish into the "pot" or corral. From there, the fish were steered into the spiller, wherein a net was raised, capturing the fish, which were then "brailed" from the net (much as one squeegees water from a window surface) by steam power into an awaiting scow that hauled them off to the cannery. The designers were aware that spawning salmon never turn back into their wakes but push forward. By 1899, a total of 12 traps were located off South Beach alone, all owned by corporations such as Pacific American Fisheries. The traps were especially adept at nabbing sockeye that gathered in eddies closer to shore and before could only be caught with seine or gillnets.

A lead extends nearly 400 yards from the camp to the fish trap at South Beach on the Strait of Juan de Fuca. The piles were removed each fall when the salmon runs were complete, so the crews learned to mark the holes. Long leads were at the heart of the controversy over the traps, the questions being how long, how many, and would the resource eventually be exhausted?

Here the trap hands spill fish into a scow via brailing, thereby completing the task they were beginning on page 103. Such traps were outlawed by 1934 as a result of pressures from sport and commercial purse seine and gillnet fishers.

South Beach, the fish trap camp, and beached dories can be seen from what is today called the Jackson Overlook. Then the view was from the front yard of the second Jakle home, which was torn down when the park was created in 1966. Liza Jakle's first son, Frank Bryant, owned the white house on 40 acres standing where the springs begin at the base of the American Camp prairie.

In another panorama, from the opposite direction, the Jakle homestead is visible on the ridge at far left, while Frank Bryant's house is almost dead center and adjacent to today's Pickett's Lane. The park's Mount Finlayson trail cuts through the homestead where the house site borders Cattle Point Road. Daffodils appear there each spring.

The lower slopes of Mount Finlayson end in crumbling bluffs that resemble high-country glacial moraines above the Strait of Juan de Fuca. The bluffs lie below the rail fence in this *c.* 1920 image. The three fish traps visible here are accurately marked on U.S. Coast Survey charts drawn from 1896 to 1898.

Fish traps, purse seine fishing boats, and a Pacific American Fisheries steamer work the straits together in this *c.* 1920s shot from Grandma's Cove on American Camp's rocky shore. Families of some of the men lived in shacks above the beach. Relations between fish trap workers and fishermen could be strained, as the fishermen believed the traps were depleting the sockeye resource.

Fish trap workers approach the beach in their dories following a shift. The initials PAF on the bows stand for Pacific American Fisheries, one of the leading commercial fishing companies in the Pacific Northwest with a large complex in Bellingham, Washington. The photograph offers a good look at a "lead" spanning from the beach to the trap. The traps could catch up to 37,000 fish per day.

A PAF fish trap crew pauses for the photographer at the South Beach camp in the early 19th century. It is a remarkable portrait of a wide range of personalities, from the rugged "lawman" type at far left to the jaunty fellow with the derby at center and the best buddies reclining below. The author's personal favorite is the fellow with the big boots and mustache seated front right. (WMHA.)

In this action shot, a tug raises the net with a steam-powered winch and also provides the power to a chain-weighted brail, which forces the fish from the net and into the scow. The workers inside the trap help the task along from their dories. The fish trap closure had a profound economic impact on Friday Harbor, which was considered a cannery worker and fisherman's town.

A brail spills a net full of sockeye salmon into a scow moored next to a fish trap off South Beach. A PAF tugboat in the background provides the power for this operation. One such rig in 1900 trapped 7,000 fish in one day, but the cannery counted only 5,500—a common discrepancy.

A PAF tug hauls the scows from trap to trap off the bluffs of South Beach. Note the men standing on the vessel to the rear of the last scow. These operations were ongoing throughout the summer months and into fall, when the salmon feed and rest in the eddies between the tides off the island's western shore on their way to spawning grounds.

The end destinations for the fish scows were canneries such as the Friday Harbor Packing Company (purchased by the PAF in 1899), which stood where the ferry landing is today in Friday Harbor. On July 9, 1900, the cannery received 2,000 fish resulting in 178 cases of sockeye, 35 cases of red spring, and 8 cases of white spring salmon. A few days later, the cannery received 5,790 sockeye and 540 spring salmon.

As the years rolled by, visitors who were curious about the dead pig that almost started a war continued to visit the military post sites—especially English Camp. Thanks to Crook's waste-not, want-not attitude, the several history structures, including the blockhouse, remained standing. In this post–World War II view, a mother and daughter chat with a personal guide, Mary Crook Davis.

Mary Crook Davis wears a 19th-century bonnet in 1959 to lend authenticity to the decaying blockhouse, on which a "Private Property" sign has been posted. By 1959, Crook's severe arthritis required the use of two canes. Mary died in an automobile accident this same year, necessitating the return to the farm in 1960 of his other widowed sister, Rhoda Crook Anderson.

Jim Crook and Rhoda Crook Anderson pose in 1966 in front of the Royal Marine forge adjacent to their home. Three years earlier, they had granted the parade ground to Washington State at the same time U.S. senator Henry M. Jackson was pushing a bill through Congress to acquire the lands from the state and create a "Pig War National Monument."

Jim Crook and Rhoda Crook Anderson appear at a 1965 public meeting in Friday Harbor, held to determine whether or not a national park was feasible for San Juan Island. Sen. Henry M. "Scoop" Jackson, D-Washington (far right), thought it was and had, with U.S. senator Warren Magnuson and U.S. representative Lloyd Meeds (both D-Washington), written legislation for its creation.

This winter view of English Camp captures the site as it appeared when the National Park Service took possession of the land in 1966. Most of the fruit trees had died and been removed by then. The gate was at the base of the hill where the family home still stands. This was the approximate view from the Royal Marine mess room.

By 1966, the Royal Marine commissary (storehouse) had a saddle-shaped roof and was on the verge of collapsing in on itself. The National Park Service dismantled the commissary, blockhouse, and surviving barracks timber by timber and rebuilt them from the ground up, saving as many historic pieces as possible.

The Royal Marine barracks seems to be undulating down to the bay in this c. 1967 shot. The National Park Service sealed this and the other structures to be reclaimed before starting work. The Crooks lived in this building off and on from 1876 and left a few surprises behind (see page 114).

The Royal Marine barracks is dismantled as part of the restoration process. In this view, the partitions added by the Crooks are bared and the salvageable boards sorted into piles. Once the foundation was cleared, archaeologists from the University of Idaho started the excavations.

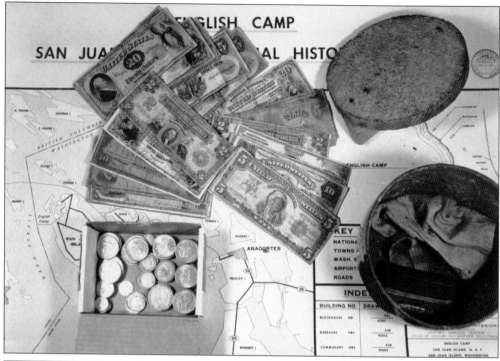

In the early 1970s, the barracks demolition crew found in the attic a Dutch oven filled with currency and gold coins. This was William Crook's "treasure," for which his son Jim hunted for more than 60 years until his death in 1967. The pot had been concealed in a panel where the attic hatch rested when open. The young Crook had opened that hatch thousands of times and never thought to look in that spot.

Historic preservation specialists remove the waterlogged and rotten lower story of the blockhouse and prepare fresh logs for restoration. The jacked-up upper story is devoid of siding, revealing the original log configuration with all six loopholes visible. The "new" base, subject to flood tides and marine parasites, was again replaced in kind in 1995 and underwent refurbishing in 2007.

At American Camp, the National Park Service evaluated the existing farm structures on the more than 1,200-acre historical park site. All of the structures were eventually razed or moved except for the one above, which was known as the McRae House for the family that had occupied it for several decades. While examining the crawl space, historic architects discovered chimney/fireplace footings that dated to the 1860s or earlier.

Realizing that the building had to have been one of the original officers' quarters on the site, archaeologists turned to the remainder of officers' row and eventually covered most of the old parade ground. In the photograph above, students from Dr. Roderick Sprague's University of Idaho archaeology classes work as part of a summer field school program from 1970 to 1979.

The University of Idaho field school also excavated the former Hudson's Bay Company site just south of the old officers' quarters. Their work revealed that the structures had indeed been of the classic HBC post-and-sill construction technique, where the dressed logs were fitted into slots in the corners.

One critical historic landscape that had to be restored was the old Hudson's Bay Company dock site on Griffin Bay. This was where Pickett landed on July 27, 1859, and where San Juan Village sprang up almost immediately. To restore the historic landscape, every structure above had to be removed or demolished, including the fence along the shoreline.

The park's first superintendent, Carl Stoddard, had the formidable task of acquiring the properties necessary to re-create the historical landscape at both park sites. He also had to establish a balance between maintaining the parklands as the playgrounds they had always been to islanders and preserving and protecting the cultural and natural resources. He was remarkably successful and was warmly welcomed back to San Juan Island on his retirement.

By the mid-1970s, American Camp's first visitor contact station was a barn-like breezeway with a two-dimensional boundary dispute exhibit and an information desk staffed by rangers and volunteers. Visitors walked through the building on their way through the trees to the historical site, which included restorations of the officers' and laundress quarters and the redoubt beyond. The station was on the site of the old Rosler farm.

Volunteers are the lifeblood of any national park and more so for a new park such as San Juan Island National Historical Park. Some of the first volunteers in 1972 were, from left to right, (first row) Janie Leche and Kim Bryant; (second row) Shelley Wiltse, Kathy Jones, NPS ranger Sydney Brown, Kelly Montgomery, and Nancy Lowe. Not pictured are Christine Settles, Paula Sundstrom, and Becky Goff.

While park volunteers saw to interpretation needs, the University of Idaho field school continued its work for the park at English Camp. In this mid-1970s image, the crews are taking a break from an excavation near the blockhouse that revealed the Royal Marine flagpole foundation. In the background, restoration crews are reassembling the commissary building.

In addition to seeking properties to restore the historic landscape, the park also sought (and continues to seek) buildings that once belonged to the military camp. The building above was located on the Peter Lawson farm and at the time was thought to be the Royal Marine hospital. It has since been moved to the English Camp parade ground, though historians suspect it was the surgeon's quarters and may belong on Officers' Hill.

When park officials finally determined that the old Warbass house was a laundress quarters, and not one of the officers' quarters as claimed, it was stripped and prepared for moving. The building was cut down to the original floor plan to conform to an archaeological site at American Camp. Compare this image with those on pages 97 and 98.

Park superintendent Carl Stoddard gives the opening address in park dedication ceremonies at English Camp in 1972. Officials from Great Britain, Canada, and the United States attended the ceremonies, which featured a vintage artillery demonstration. Postal enthusiasts also purchased a special cancellation done on-site.

The newly restored buildings were in pristine condition in 1972 for the dedication ceremonies and have weathered well over the years. The Royal Marine barracks now double as a visitor contact station during the summer months. Twice a year, the park hosts dances featuring period music and steps, as was done during the joint military occupation.

Direct descendants of George Pickett have twice visited San Juan Island to learn more about their famous ancestor's West Coast life. Here George Pickett III, a decorated World War I veteran, listens carefully while a curator talks about his grandfather's house in Bellingham. Pickett also walked the ramparts at American Camp and was exuberantly feted by Friday Harbor citizens.

George Pickett's great-grandson, Christiancy "Chris" Pickett of Salt Lake City, arrived on San Juan Island on July 27, 1972, to help the National Park Service officially dedicate the San Juan National Historical Park. Pickett participated in all of the festivities, including the dedication at English Camp, and then took a moment to pose in front of the park office in front of the famous headline.

Rhoda Crook Anderson greets a park visitor from the kitchen of her home in the early 1970s. When the National Park Service took possession of the last 170 acres of Crook land, Anderson was granted permission to occupy the house overlooking the parade ground for as long as she wished to stay. She died in 1972.

U.S. Second District representative Al Swift, D-Washington (far left), visits the formal garden at English Camp in the 1980s. As with Senator Jackson before him, Swift took a special interest in the park. In the background, the steps to Officers' Hill are undergoing rehabilitation. The Royal Marines installed the limestone steps at the base, which were rehabilitated and supplemented with granite stones on the upper portion of the stairway in 2005.

Helen Jackson accepts a framed photograph from then–NPS Pacific Northwest director Charles Odegaard. Behind them is a memorial erected to the memory of her husband, Senator Jackson, who was a driving force in creating San Juan Island National Historical Park. Jackson died in 1983. The park held a special place in Jackson's heart not only because it represented peace, but also because it was the scene of many happy occasions with his wife and family. The presentation was held in the mid-1980s.

Senator Jackson poses with his children for his wife, Helen, in this c. 1972 image from a family outing to San Juan Island. The garden was installed to commemorate the 100th anniversary of Kaiser Wilhelm's decision and was intended to duplicate the original down to the 19th-century London design.

A park maintenance crew poses behind the Jackson Memorial they installed in the mid-1980s. The site, now called the Jackson Overlook, offers a stunning view of South Beach, the dunes, the American Camp prairie, and the Olympic Mountains (see page 105, top).

Jim Crook, identifiable by his canes, accompanies two visitors up the old Military Road trail at the base of Young Hill at English Camp. The man to his left is possibly U.S. senator Warren Magnuson, D-Washington, who in the early 1960s wrote an article about the Pig War for *American Heritage* magazine. Magnuson and Senator Jackson cosponsored the bill to create a "Pig War National Historical Park." The name was changed to San Juan Island National Historical Park as the legislation advanced through Senate and House to be signed into law in 1966 by Pres. Lyndon B. Johnson. The legacy of Senators Jackson and Magnuson, Congressman Meeds, Jim Crook, R. Lambert Baynes, Geoffrey Phipps Hornby, Winfield Scott, and even George Pickett (once he figured things out) lives on in a place where individuals and nations resolved their problems peacefully without resorting to violence.

BIBLIOGRAPHY

PRIMARY SOURCES:

National Archives of the United States
National Archives of the United Kingdom of Great Britain
National Archives of Canada

(For a complete list of primary sources for this work, see www.nps.gov/sajh/historyculture/the-pig-war-bibliography.)

STUDIES:

Thompson, Erwin N. *Historic Resource Study: San Juan Island NHP*. MMS. San Juan Island National Historical Park, Friday Harbor, Washington, 1972.
Wray, Jacilee. *The Salmon Bank: An Ethnohistoric Compilation*. Port Angeles, WA: Olympic National Park/San Juan Island National Historical Park, 2003.

BOOKS:

Eardly-Wilmot S., Lt., ed. *Our Journal of the Pacific by the Officers of H.M.S. Zealous*. London: Longmans, Green, and Company, 1873.
Edgerton, Mrs. Fred. *Admiral of the Fleet, Sir Geoffrey Phipps Hornby*. Edinburgh, 1896.
Gough, Barry. *The Royal Navy and the Northwest Coast of North America, 1810–1814*. Vancouver, B.C.: University of British Columbia, 1971.
Hill, J. R., ed. *Oxford Illustrated History of the Royal Navy*. Oxford: Oxford University Press, 1995.
Norman, Francis Martin. *"Martello Tower" in China and the Pacific in H.M.S. "Tribune" 1856–60*. London: George Allen, 1902.
Stein, Julie K. *Exploring Coast Salish Prehistory: The Archaeology of San Juan Island*. Seattle: University of Washington Press, 2000.
Vouri, Michael. *The Pig War: Standoff on Griffin Bay*. Friday Harbor, WA: Griffin Bay Bookstore, 1999.
————. *Outpost of Empire: The Royal Marines and the Joint Occupation of San Juan Island*. Seattle: Northwest Interpretive Association/University of Washington, 2004.

INDEX

ACROSS AMERICA, PEOPLE ARE DISCOVERING SOMETHING WONDERFUL. *THEIR HERITAGE.*

Arcadia Publishing is the leading local history publisher in the United States. With more than 4,000 titles in print and hundreds of new titles released every year, Arcadia has extensive specialized experience chronicling the history of communities and celebrating America's hidden stories, bringing to life the people, places, and events from the past. To discover the history of other communities across the nation, please visit:

www.arcadiapublishing.com

Customized search tools allow you to find regional history books about the town where you grew up, the cities where your friends and family live, the town where your parents met, or even that retirement spot you've been dreaming about.